The Gift of Life

Ari Idee

The Gift of Life by Ari Idee

Copyright © 2014 Technology and Imagination Press
Text and Illustrations copyright © 2014 by Ari Idee
All rights reserved.

No part of this publication may be reproduced, stored in a retrieval system, or transmitted in any form or by any means, electronic, mechanical, photocopying, recording, or otherwise, without written permission of the publisher.
For information, on getting permission for reprints and excerpts, contact tip_books@happyhippocreations.com

ISBN: 0-9798991-7-6
ISBN-13: 978-0-9798991-7-1

First Printing 2014

The Gift of Life

Ari Idee

Introduction

In the ancient days, Jewish people lived in their Hebrew Kingdom to the southeast of the Mediterranean Sea. About 2000 years ago, the Ancient Roman Empire overcame and destroyed this Kingdom. The Roman government and soldiers dispersed so many of the Jewish people, who then scattered all over what would become modern Europe.

Over the centuries, in the Christian countries, Jewish people were always cast out of society because they had a different religion. Judaism is their religion. Many centuries ago, under Roman rule, the Jewish leaders had been one of the local governments. They had ruled Jerusalem at the time that Jesus of Nazareth was judged, and so the Jewish people had the reputation among Christians as "the killers of Christ."

Without their own country – and by law not allowed to own property – the Jewish people relied on education. They made tremendous efforts to educate their children. Education was a fortune that had no weight for them as they relocated from time to time. Because of their educational efforts, Jewish people had great success in the fields of science, music, and business. Consequently, many Jewish people did become wealthy.

Adolf Hitler, the leader of Nazi Germany, blamed the Jewish people for the bad economy in the worldwide financial crisis of that time. With his charisma, Hitler told Germans that they were suffering poverty because the Jewish people had taken all the important jobs from them. Hitler worked on the anxiety and paranoia of the German people and, with his strong government policies, taught them to hate the Jewish people. Regular, normal, middle-class German citizens – and even good-natured and optimistic citizens – were overpowered and became pawns in Hitler's scheme. If any individual or group took a stand against Hitler, his same government would find them and ostracize them, just as separation and the specter of death hung over the Jewish people.

In 1935, Nazi Germany signed the Nuremberg Laws. These laws stripped Jewish people of their citizenship in Germany. Jewish people had to wear a yellow Star of David on their clothes. They were no longer allowed to ride on trains, in cars, or on bicycles. They were excluded from all public facilities. Visiting their German friends or any Christian people was illegal for the Jews. They had to shop only in Jewish shops from 3:00pm to 5:00pm. Their curfew was 8:00pm. They were forbidden to stay outside after that time, even in their own backyard.

As early as 1938, over 10,000 Jewish people were expelled from Germany. They became refugees again, as they had been throughout history. But the worst thing came when, in 1940, Nazis started hunting Jewish people to send them to concentration camps, that were used as extermination camps, such as one named Auschwitz in Poland.

Chiune Sugihara was a Japanese consul living in Lithuania during this turbulent period. The Japanese government wanted to align with Germany. Mr. Sugihara was about to face to the most difficult decision of his life.

As a consul, a representative of his government overseas, he was supposed to be a good Japanese model citizen, and obey every rule of his superiors. However, he chose to disobey the Japanese Government risking even his own life to the Nazis.

Chapter 1

The Republic of Lithuania is the largest and most southern country of the three Baltic States (Lithuania, Latvia and Estonia), that face the Baltic Sea. Lithuania's second largest city, Kaunas, is a quiet and historic town, located nearly in the exact center of this country.

In the summer of 1939, a Japanese family moved into Kaunas, Lithuania, because the father of the family, Chiune Sugihara, was an acting consul at the Consulate General of Japan in that city.

They were the first Japanese who had ever arrived in Kaunas. People in Kaunas were curious about this family. The local newspaper wrote a special feature about Japanese life and culture from their interview with Chiune. Kaunas people were very happy to welcome this consul to their country because he was answering their questions seriously and sincerely.

The Sugihara family's arrival made a big Japanese boom in quiet Kaunas. The Lithuanian people enjoyed thinking about and imagining these formerly unknown to them islands of Japan.

However, those first peaceful days were fading fast due to a war between Germany and the

Soviet Union. From 1933 to 1945, Germany was called "Nazi Germany." German people believed that they were the best example of perfect human beings, and all other people were not as good on their scale of pure to impure. Their unfortunate belief was that Jewish people were the worst. The Nazi German government's policy started the persecution of Jewish people.

Chapter 2

Nazi Germany invaded Poland in the Fall of 1939. This became the trigger to start World War II. Lithuania got caught in the war because it was located right between Nazi Germany and the Soviet Union. The Soviet Union required the Baltic States – Lithuania, Estonia and Latvia – to build Soviet military bases to station their soldiers.

In front of the Soviet massive military power, the Baltic states had no choice but to comply with their demands. The most important thing for these three countries was to avoid bloodshed of their own people in the coming battles. The Baltic States formed an alliance with the Soviet Union in 1940. Now, Lithuania was filled with Soviet soldiers. It was no longer a quiet historically quaint country. Lithuania was over-run by the Soviet Union.

Mr. Sugihara told his family, "Lithuania is no longer an independent country. This consulate will be closed down soon." He meant to tell his wife and children that soon they would relocate to Berlin.

On the morning of July 18, 1940, not so long after the Baltic alliance with the Soviet Union, the Sugihara family was wakened by the murmuring of a crowd outside of their home. Mr. Sugihara went to the window and, drawing the drapes back, he gaped out at hundreds of people milling around in front of the consulate. These people were some of the Jews who had fled from Poland. Nazi Germany was chasing and catching the Jewish people in Poland to send them to a concentration camp. Just because they were Jewish, very many men and women, and even children, were gathered in this concentration camp called Auschwitz, to eventually be killed.

Chapter 3

Jewish people who were fortunate enough to escape from Poland traveled to Lithuania, and then had managed to reach Kaunas. Sugihara gazed in anguish at those refugees outside his window. He knew what they wanted – visas to go to Japan. However, Japan was then trying to create an alliance with Germany and Italy. If Sugihara were to help these people escape from Nazi Germany, it would be considered a hostile act on the part of the Japanese by the Nazis. While Sugihara was worrying about how to deal with the situation, more and more Jewish people kept arriving to crowd the street in front of the consulate.

Sugihara decided to talk to them. He asked the Jewish people to choose five representatives to talk with him. On July the 19th, the five chosen leaders entered Sugihara's office. A man named Zerach Warhaftig started talking, "We are trying to escape from being hunted down by the Nazis. Please let us escape through Japan, and then we can go somewhere else."

Sugihara answered, "I can issue a couple of visas. However, I cannot do that for hundreds. I have to get permission from the Ministry of Foreign

Affairs in Japan to issue so many."

Sugihara sent many telegrams to Japan over the next week asking for guidance in this situation, but the answer was always the same – very cold: "Without a prepared entry visa for a traveler's destination country, Japan cannot issue any visa for anyone, not Jewish, Lithuanian, nor Polish." The Jewish people were clearly refugees, and did not have the required entry visas to other countries. Sugihara suffered in deep sympathy with those waiting Jewish people.

Chiune Sugihara spent two nights thinking deeply about the situation. He called in his wife, Yukiko, and spoke to her, "I will issue visas for those Jews. I will disobey the Ministry of Foreign Affairs. Is that okay for you?" Yukiko considered the possible consequences and then nodded. He continued, "Even if I were to be so unlucky as to be arrested by the Nazi Government, I believe they wouldn't go so far as to hurt you and the children."

Since he decided to help, he prepared to issue visas for numerous people. He asked the consulate of The Soviet Union to allow Jews to pass through to Japan.

On the 29th of July, 1940, Sugihara was ready to accept refugees into his office.

Chapter 4

Early in the morning ten days after his talk with the five representatives Sugihara went outside and, standing near the gate in the high fence surrounding the consulate, announced, "I will issue transit visas for you all to go to Japan." The crowd fell silent in disbelief at first and then reacted in a variety of ways to this new hope. Some screamed in joy. Mothers held their children tightly. Old people prayed to God. Strangers hugged each other.

Sugihara started handwriting the transit visas one by one. The people formed a long, long line and snaked into his office to receive their gift of life. The people were moved to tears and some got on their knees and tried to kiss his shoes. Sugihara gently made them stand up and gave them words of encouragement. "The world is like a gigantic wheel. All of us are part of it and we have to hold hands to make the wheel go round without friction or disputes."

The usual business hours of the consulate were from 9:00am to 2:00pm. However, Sugihara kept on writing the visas until midnight. He issued about three hundred visas on this first day. He wired the Ministry of Foreign Affairs in Japan that he had started issuing visas for the Jewish people. The answer he got from Japan was to stop and to immediately move out of the consulate building.

Sugihara ignored that order and kept issuing visas for days. The normal visa issuing procedure was that for each visa he should report that he had issued it to the Ministry of Foreign Affairs. However, Sugihara stopped reporting the numbers after he had already issued 2000 visas. He even stopped charging the visa fee. He had no time to deal with bureaucratic procedures. After all, he was performing a mission to issue as many visas as he could, in total solitude.

Chiune Sugihara's decision to take the responsibility and to write visas for the refugee Jewish people was a tremendous act of disobedience for a government employee – and a citizen – in Japanese society. He was just a small cog in the huge machine called the Foreign Ministry. Sugihara was supposed to do anything and everything that he was ordered to do. But now, he had started to move on his own – to take the initiative – to go against the flow. He jumped off the cogwheel. He would surely lose his job. He would also lose the safety and comfort of being a recognized member of the community in Japanese society. Even in the privacy of his own home, even with his numbed arms, he couldn't let his wife help with any part of writing the visas. If he did, he was afraid, it would bring trouble to her, too. He expected trouble, but Sugihara couldn't risk his wife who was the mother of three young children. For the Jewish people – and for the sake of his own family's future – he had to cope with disobeying his government and "betters" and do this act totally alone.

Chapter 5

Consul Sugihara had been hand writing visas without taking very much time to eat or sleep for more than twenty days. His single excellent fountain pen broke from overuse. He got dark circles under his eyes. His arms were numb. He was reaching the limits of his physical abilities.

"Shall I stop? Even if I work hard, I can't help all the Jewish people waiting outside the consulate. So many more are still coming. I can help only a small percentage of them," Sugihara found himself muttering one night.

Yukiko asked him sincerely, "Please, keep writing. There are so many desperate people waiting for you. I beg you. Write as many visas as you can." Yukiko couldn't help begging her husband even though she saw how worn out he was. Every day she was peeking through their curtains at Jewish mothers with their young children. Their eyes cried out for help. Because she was also a mother, Yukiko couldn't do anything but plead with her husband to help save their lives.

Sugihara smiled at Yukiko. He felt that he knew that his wife would say that. "I will," Sugihara nodded as he went back to writing with his second best pen. What's more, he knew for himself that he could not stop.

On August the 28th, the Ministry of Foreign Affairs in Japan sent him the "final" order to move out of the consulate. Sugihara decided to close the consulate at noon on that day. He asked his friend at the Japanese consulate in Moscow, Russia, to issue transit visas for Jewish people. As he and his family exited the consulate, he put a notice on the door saying that Jewish people could receive visas from the Japanese consulate in Moscow. After the Japanese consulate in Kaunas was closed, many Jewish refugees actually did get visas in Moscow to escape to Japan. Sugihara also wrote on the notice the name and address of the hotel he would be staying in for a couple of days until he must finally leave for Berlin. Some of the most desperate people rushed to follow him to the hotel. Since Sugihara was closing the consulate, he had to return the official consulate stamp, so he couldn't issue official visas. He hand wrote "passage permits" for the desperate people instead of visas.

Chapter 6

On September the first, the Sugihara family boarded the train for Berlin. Numerous Jewish people were at the Kaunas railway station. There were some people there who just thanked Sugihara but there were also others who desperately needed passage permits. Even as he was sitting in his seat on the train, Sugihara kept writing permits, as many as he could. He was deeply absorbed in writing as fast as he could. He was throwing permits through the train window to the numerous people waiting on the platform.

The whistle blew to signal that the train would be leaving in a moment. Sugihara raised his face up with a terrible, agonizing look. He stood up from his seat and, speaking out the window to the crowd, said, "Please, forgive me, everyone. The train is leaving now and I cannot write any more travel permits. I wish you all the best." As the train engine started to roar, the Assistant Consul Sugihara bowed deeply to the crowd.

Then the train started moving. "Thank you, Mr. Sugihara!" someone shouted. One young man started running along beside the slowly moving train. With tears streaming down his face, he shouted to the departing consul, "Mr. Sugihara! We will never forget you! We will survive and meet with you again!" That young man was Jehoshua Nishri, one of the five Jewish representatives who had pleaded for the lives of the refugees with Sugihara on July the 19th. Nishri kept running and shouting his message over and over again until he came to the end of the platform and the accelerating train pulled ahead of him.

Chapter 7

After the Sugihara family arrived in Berlin, they wandered from place to place in Europe. They moved four times in six years with their three children. Their first move was from Kuanas, Lithuania to Berlin, Germany. Then they moved from Berlin to Prague in the Czech Republic, and from Prague to Konigsberg in East Prussia, and finally from Konigsberg to Bucharest in Rumania.

On December 8, 1941, Japan attacked Pearl Harbor in Hawaii, a group of islands in the Pacific Ocean that were American territory. As a result of this surprise attack by the Japanese military more than two thousand Americans died. The American government declared war on Japan and entered the European war with England against Nazi Germany and Italy. War quickly spread throughout the entire world. The Allies – America, England, France, Russia and China – and the Axis Powers – Nazi Germany, Japan and Italy – were the two main sides of the war, but many other countries were involved in the battles.

Sugihara believed firmly that Japan and Nazi Germany would lose the war. As he predicted, Nazi Germany was gradually losing its vigor. On April

30, 1945, Hitler committed suicide. Consequently, without his leadership, Nazi Germany was easily overthrown. About four months later, the Japanese government accepted the Potsdam Declaration to surrender.

      Former Consul Sugihara and his family were caught by the Soviet Army and taken prisoner in Romania. They lost everything in a single night. Since Sugihara spoke fluent Russian, he worked in the prisoner camp as an interpreter. The family was sent from one camp to another. At least the family was together. After spending a year and a half in the camps, they were finally ordered to go back to Japan.

Chapter 8

In February of 1947, the Sugihara family returned to Japan. It had been nine and half years since they left Japan to travel to Kaunas for Mr. Sugihara's work. They happily and joyfully celebrated their safe return.

However, the harsh realities of the devastation of the war and the consequences of his solo actions hit Sugihara one after another. Soon after they had returned to Japan, Sugihara was summoned to the office of the Ministry of Foreign Affairs.

The Vice Minister of Foreign Affairs declared to him in that interview that there was no post – or any place in the Ministry – for Sugihara who had so blatantly disobeyed their orders. "I understand," was all he could say. Sugihara gave the Vice-Minister a low bow and left the office for the last time.

At home, he did not talk much about his forced resignation. Actually, he was more deeply hurt by the malicious rumors that were circulating about him than the forced resignation. There were rumors at the ministry that Sugihara had squirreled away a fortune he had made from being paid a lot for writing those visas for the Jewish refugees. This rumor was like wildfire among the workers in the Foreign Ministry. Jealousy toward the formerly distinguished diplomat fed this talk like poison created from ill intentions. People whispered that Sugihara had even opened a Swiss National Bank account with an enormous sum, all of which he had swindled from those thousands of Jewish people.

Even as Sugihara heard those ugly rumors, he held his head high and consistently observed a dignified silence. He never talked, not even with his family, about his career in the Ministry of Foreign Affairs. He held his career and all the memories he might have had as a diplomat in his own mind. But, as a wife can do, Yukiko felt and knew her husband's sorrow in his perfect silent solitude.

Chapter 9

For Sugihara, who had worked as a respectable diplomat for ten years throughout Europe, it was difficult to begin all over again in Japan. His family was in extreme financial distress. They were so hard pressed that sometimes they couldn't even buy enough to eat.

However, an additional tragedy hit the family. One day, his youngest son suddenly complained of a headache and, within several days, he had passed away. He was only seven. His young life had been taken by a particularly virulent form of leukemia all too quickly. Sugihara was overwhelmed by despair. What gave him even more heartache was that he couldn't give his young son an adequate funeral.

Chiune Sugihara was able to procure various jobs – as an interpreter for many trading firms, as a Russian language teacher, and as a Russian translator. During all the time that he was working, in all of the various makeshift jobs, he never talked with anyone about himself and his life as a Japanese diplomat.

Chapter 10

In August of 1968, Chiune Sugihara was summoned to the Israeli Embassy in Tokyo. They asked him to come to the Embassy as soon as he could. Luckily, he had just returned to Tokyo from Moscow where he had been doing his translation work. He agreed and hurried to visit the Embassy that same day.

As soon as he arrived, an elderly Jewish man standing there, waiting, recognized him. The man rushed up to him, grasping in his hand a raggedy and worn-out, hand-written paper.

"Do you remember this?" the man asked Sugihara, holding the tattered paper out to him. Tears were already rolling down the man's wrinkled face. "At the station, I am the one who promised you that I would survive and see you again."

The whole chaotic scene of the departure of the Sugihara family from Kaunas station came back to the former consul immediately and vividly. He remembered that he had been throwing visas desperately to people through the window of the train. And he also remembered that when he had to say that he couldn't write any more he stood up and bowed reverently to the crowd from the moving train. And in his mind's eye he saw and heard all the Jewish people who were crying and thanking him. He even remembered that one special young man who was shouting at the top of his voice, over and over, "Thank you. Thank you, Mr. Sugihara! We will never forget you! We surely will survive and I will see you again!" The young man even ran on the platform alongside the moving train continuing to thank Sugihara again and again. The young man's voice and his face that had been soaked with tears then now became the tear-soaked face of the man standing in front of him. Sugihara searched these memories and finally, "You are……Nishri?" he whispered in wonder.

Jehoshua Nishri had been one of the five Jewish representatives who originally had been in that meeting in the office on July 19, 1940. They had begged and pleaded with Sugihara to issue visas to the desperate Jewish people. And he was here now, holding both of Sugihara's hands firmly and warmly.

"I found you. I have been searching for you for a long, long time." Nishri hugged him and Sugihara hugged him back. They didn't need words as they cried on each other's shoulders. After 28 years, Nishri finally was able to fulfill his promise. The living warmth of their hands told them that they were together again, existing and living together beneath the same sun.

Chapter 11

Nishri started talking, "Mr. Sugihara, we have been searching for you for a long time. Thanks to your visas, so many of us could go through Japan and start our new life in the United States, Canada, Australia and other countries. Your visas saved more than 6000 Jews. Each of us has kept your precious visa. It is important to each of us because it symbolizes how we, thanks to you, can have our lives."

This was the first time Sugihara was able to know the fate of all of those Jewish people after he left Kaunas. He had scribbled out so many visas and now they were not an idea – they were people, families of men and women and children who lived because of his courage. This news poured into Sugihara's heart. They had survived! And not only survived. They had families and now were living safely with their children and even grandchildren.

Nishri also told Sugihara how difficult it had been to search for him. Right after World War II some of those Jews that he had saved had immediately started searching for him. Faithful Jewish people worked very hard in all parts of the world in order to repay the consul's kindnesses. They called the Japanese Ministry of Foreign Affairs first. However, those clerks and consuls answering their request for information gave them a cold, official Japanese Ministry answer, "There is no diplomat named Sempo Sugihara in our office."

Since Sugihara's first name had been difficult for Europeans to pronounce, he nicknamed himself "Sempo" – the Chinese reading instead of the Japanese reading of the Chinese ideographs making up his name, "Chiune." Jewish people asked the Ministry of Foreign Affairs about him by the name they knew him by, "Sempo Sugihara" and the answer was always, "Sempo Sugihara doesn't exist. There never has been anyone in the Ministry with the name of Sempo Sugihara." During the war, and after the war was over, there had been only three workers named "Sugihara" in the office. Most Japanese people should have easily understood Chiune Sugihara may have used the kanji's Chinese pronunciation of his given name.

The warm reunion with Nishri started to defrost Sugihara's stiff feelings toward his past career. Now he could know that, "What I did was not in vain." When he returned home that evening, he continued to melt, muttering to himself, "It worked. I could help them. They were saved."

Chapter 12

In 1969, Sugihara was invited to visit the state of Israel on his way to Moscow for his work. The invitation came from the Jewish people who survived by the visas that he had written. Many of those people had made their way from Japan to the new state of Israel, and became the stalwarts of the new country.

When Sugihara's plane landed in Israel, the nation's Minister of Religion welcomed him. The Minister asked the perplexed Sugihara, "Do you remember me?" then he answered the question forming in Sugihara's mind, "I was one of Jewish representatives who talked to you at the consulate in Kaunas." Sugihara gasped. He couldn't say anything for a long moment. Zerach Warhaftig, one of the five leaders who had implored Sugihara to issue visas for the Jewish people, was now Israel's Minister of Religion and was standing facing Sugihara again.

Warhaftig took Sugihara to Yad Vashem, Israel's official memorial to the Jewish victims of the Holocaust. This is the one place in the world to mourn all of the Jewish people who were killed by the Nazis during World War II. Sugihara was the first Asian who had ever been invited there.

Warhaftig awarded Sugihara a decoration and honor while they were in that holy place.

During their talk, Warhaftig found out for the first time that Sugihara had issued all of those visas to the Jewish people on his own authority. He also learned that the Japanese government had clearly and strictly opposed Sugihara's actions and that Sugihara had acted totally on his own judgement.

Warhaftig was shocked. He asked Sugihara what had been the action of the Ministry of Foreign Affairs of Japan toward him. "Did they rebuke you, Sir?" Sugihara told him that he had been simply fired after the end of the war. He smiled at Warhaftig and told of his recollections about the days he was even selling light bulbs door to door, or the time he spent as a clerk at a general store. Warhaftig was confused. He couldn't understand why Sugihara had helped the Jewish people if he knew that he was sacrificing his own career as a diplomat.

"Why? Why did you do that?" Warhaftig couldn't help asking him.

"Why?" Sugihara smiled. "Because we are same human beings."

Chapter 13

During the Israel trip in 1969, Sugihara planted a tree in the garden of Yad Vashem. It would grow big and tell people that there was a courageous Japanese diplomat. When Sugihara returned to Japan, he told his wife, Yukiko, about the engraved words, "Remember, don't forget," exhibited at Yad Vashem. This is the exact same message that every Jewish person also carves into his or her heart. Those words of Nishri continued to echo in Chiune Sugihara's mind, "Thank you Sugihara! We will never forget you! We surely will survive and I will see you again!" Sugihara and Yukiko remembered the sound of young Nishri's voice. And they remembered his words with reverence for the idea that the Jewish people carry out their word and keep their promises, no matter the difficulty they might find in doing so.

Warhaftig was even more deeply impressed by Sugihara's choices and actions when he found out the Japanese man's reasons. He worked extremely hard within the Israeli government so that it would fittingly recognize Sugihara for his bravery in the face of his own culture and society.

Finally, in 1985, the Israeli government presented Chiune (Sempo) Sugihara the highest award of honor in Israel, "Righteous Among the Nations." Since, at that time, Sugihara was confined to bed by a terrible sickness, Yukiko accepted this wonderful award for him by traveling to Israel.

After coming back to Japan, Yukiko told Sugihara how busy the presentation had been with reporters and journalists of all the media around the world, and how well-known he was outside of Japan. Sugihara smiled and said "What I did was not something to be made much of. All I did was something commonplace." From the worldwide publicity spilling into their country, the Japanese people found out for the first time ever that there had been a courageous Japanese diplomat who saved over 6000 people from sure death at the hands of the Nazis in World War II. Slowly it dawned on them exactly what he had done and they started admiring his unselfish act.

On July 31, 1989, Chiune Sugihara lifted his earthly veil and – satisfied that in the eyes of the world and even his own countrymen he had been vindicated for his acts – finished his eighty-six year old life.

Chapter 14

In 1999, a postage stamp with Sugihara's portrait was issued in Israel. Outside of Japan, he was honored and respected for his choice to help those people to escape certain death. Following Israel's lead, Japan also created a stamp with his portrait. Finally, the Japanese people began to really know about Sugihara's totally selfless work during World War II and, more importantly, their admiration of his integrity could grow and grow.

In 2001, the Minister of Foreign Affairs in Japan called for a press conference at which a high authority of the agency made a formal apology to Yukiko and his children about their official "rudeness" toward Sugihara while he had still been alive. By "rudeness" they meant not only his preemptive firing but also the malicious rumors they had allowed to circulate and run rampant in the office where he had been working for such a brief period after the war – the rumors that he had made lots of money by selling visas to thousands of Jewish people.

Fourteen years after his death, Sugihara's honor was finally recovered – officially – in Japanese society. Sugihara's nobile acts had given life to so many Jewish refugees and showed how the courage of one man to act in accord with his faith could be a beacon of light to people around the world.

Nishri's voice called out not only his promise to remember and to meet again, but the promise that we all – as humans – have to keep in mind: "Thank you, Mr. Sempo Sugihara. We will never forget you."

Acknowledgements

Decision, Visas for Lives, Masakatsu Watanabe. Taisho Shuppan 1996.

Story of Chiune Sugihara by Yukiko Sugihara and Hiroki Sugihara. Kin no Hoshisha 2011.

Sugihara Chiune, Masakatsu Watanabe and Sayori Abe. Shogakukan 2001.

Visas for 6,000 Lives, Ando Tomio and Smadar Moise. Sanyusha 2013.

Ari Idee was born in Japan in 1976. She graduated with a B.A. in Art from Ueno Gakuen University in 1999 and a B.A. in English Literature from Meiji Gakuin Unversity in 2003.

Books by Ari Idee:
What's Your Snack?
Delicious Japan by Month
Great Peacemaker

http://aribooks.com

Editor: Salle Hayden at www.upstartservices.com
"Notes from Further West 5 1/2 Years in Japan"
"6 Books in Search of a Point"

www.ingramcontent.com/pod-product-compliance
Lightning Source LLC
Chambersburg PA
CBHW041812040426
42450CB00001B/16